WILD *about* SEAFOOD

Stoeger Publishing
Great Outdoor Books Since 1925

STOEGER PUBLISHING COMPANY
is a division of Benelli U.S.A.

Benelli U.S.A.
Vice President and General Manager: Stephen Otway
Director of Brand Marketing and Communications:
  Stephen McKelvain

Stoeger Publishing Company
President: Jeffrey Reh
Publisher: Jay Langston
Managing Editor: Harris J. Andrews
Design and Production Director: Cynthia T. Richardson
Director of Photography: Alex Bowers
Imaging Specialist: William Graves
Publishing Assistant: Christine Lawton
National Sales Manager: Jennifer Thomas
Sales Manager Assistant: Julie Brownlee
Assistant to the Publisher: Shannon McWilliams
Translation: Katrin Sermat

© 2004 by Stoeger Publishing Company. All rights reserved.

No part of this book may be reproduced or transmitted in any
form or by any means, electronic or mechanical, including
photocopying, recording, or by any information storage and
retrieval system, without permission in writing from the Publisher.

Published by Stoeger Publishing Company
17603 Indian Head Highway, Suite 200
Accokeek, Maryland 20607

BK0405
ISBN:0-88317-259-3
Library of Congress Control Number: 2002110164

Manufactured in the United States of America.

Distributed to the book trade and
to the sporting goods trade by:
Stoeger Industries
17603 Indian Head Highway, Suite 200
Accokeek, Maryland 20607

Fifth in the *Wild About* cookbooks series.

Printed in China.

OTHER PUBLICATIONS:
Shooter's Bible 2004 - 95th Edition
  The World's Standard Firearms Reference Book
Gun Trader's Guide - 26th Edition
  Complete, Fully Illustrated Guide to Modern
  Firearms with Current Market Values

Hunting & Shooting
  Hounds of the World
  The Turkey Hunter's Tool Kit: Shooting Savvy
  Archer's Bible
  Hunting Whitetails East & West
  Mr. Whitetail's Trailing the Hunter's Moon
  Hunting Club Management Guide
  Complete Book of Whitetail Hunting
  Hunting and Shooting with the Modern Bow
  The Ultimate in Rifle Accuracy
  Advanced Black Powder Hunting
  Labrador Retrievers
  Hunting America's Wild Turkey
  Taxidermy Guide
  Cowboy Action Shooting
  Great Shooters of the World

Collecting Books
  Sporting Collectibles
  The Working Folding Knife
  The Lore of Spices

Firearms
  Antique Guns
  P-38 Automatic Pistol
  The Walther Handgun Story
  Complete Guide to Service Handguns
  Firearms Disassembly with Exploded Views
  Rifle Guide
  Gunsmithing at Home
  The Book of the Twenty-Two
  Complete Guide to Modern Rifles
  Complete Guide to Classic Rifles
  Legendary Sporting Rifles
  FN Browning Armorer to the World
  Modern Beretta Firearms
  How to Buy & Sell Used Guns
  Heckler & Koch: Armorers of the Free World
  Spanish Handguns

Reloading
  The Handloader's Manual of Cartridge
    Conversions
  Modern Sporting Rifle Cartridges
  Complete Reloading Guide

Fishing
  Ultimate Bass Boats
  Bassing Bible
  The Flytier's Companion
  Deceiving Trout
  The Complete Book of Trout Fishing
  The Complete Book of Flyfishing
  Peter Dean's Guide to Fly-Tying
  The Flytier's Manual
  Handbook of Fly Tying
  The Fly Fisherman's Entomological Pattern Book
  Fiberglass Rod Making
  To Rise a Trout

Motorcycles & Trucks
  The Legend of Harley-Davidson
  The Legend of the Indian
  Best of Harley-Davidson
  Classic Bikes
  Great Trucks
  4X4 Vehicles

Cooking Game
  Fish & Shellfish Care & Cookery
  Game Cookbook
  Dress 'Em Out
  Wild About Venison
  Wild About Game Birds
  Wild About Freshwater Fish
  Wild About Waterfowl
  World's Best CatFish Cook Book

Contents

Introduction

Water is the earth's lifeblood. For humans, as for all creatures, there is no existence without water in some form. We live on a water planet — water covers three-quarters of the globe, most of it the saltwater of the great oceans. The seas nurture and nourish us in countless ways. One of the most delightful forms of that sustenance comes from the ocean's bounty of fish, shellfish and crustaceans.

From our earliest history mankind has forged a vital bond with the restless seas. Fish were caught in a wide variety of ways guided by man's inventiveness and ingenuity. They were netted, speared, caught by hand and by hook, trapped and harvested in other manners. Man fashioned and improved boats over countless generations and gradually increased their size and seaworthiness and the seas became a seemingly inexhaustible larder. The dangers and uncertainties associated with capturing its bounty seemed well worthwhile. Whether it was spawning runs of salmon caught with dip nets and dried in the sun, barrels filled with salted cod hooked off the Grand Banks, flatfish caught in the shallows and back bays, or deep-sea tuna iced in the hold of a trawler, the seas have figured prominently in the diet of coastal dwellers throughout the world.

Shellfish quickly became a staple of human diet thanks to the fact that they could be taken with less danger and often with less effort. In tidal mud flats and back bays, in the mouths and estuaries of countless creeks and rivers, mussels, clams and oysters were there for the taking. In many cases they required no more effort than waiting for low tide to expose mud flats and shellfish beds. Crustaceans usually required more effort, but the wonderfully rich taste and nourishment afforded by shrimp and lobsters made them a dietary staple. Even today, the demand for lobster supports coastal fishermen and entire economies in some maritime regions.

We are belatedly and somewhat painfully coming to the realization that the bounty of the sea is not inexhaustible. Over fishing in various ways, most notably long lining and the use of huge nets capable of hauling in everything that swims, have taken their toll. One needs only to ponder the sad story of the Grand Banks' cod or greatly reduced salmon runs of the Atlantic and Pacific Northwest to realize as much. Pollution, a by-product of human population growth, has done tremendous damage as well.

Yet the undeniable fact remains that the bounty of the seas offers us wonderful variety of foods. Health specialists are increasingly aware of the benefits of a diet in which seafood figures prominently. The following recipes are a celebration of the sea's bounty, and offer expert guidance on how to create the sort of irresistible fare sure to tickle the palate of any gourmet.

Before we move on to the heart of this book—dozens of recipes for preparing fish, shellfish and crustaceans—perhaps a few practical suggestions on selecting and caring for the sea's offerings are in order.

1. Freshness should always be foremost when choosing seafood. Select fish with firm flesh and little odor and keep in mind the fact that cooking anything from the sea as soon as possible means retaining maximum flavor.
2. When freezing fish, shellfish or crustaceans, try to remove as much air as possible from the container (vacuum sealing is recommended where possible). Do not keep frozen for long periods of time.
3. Whether you do the cleaning or have it done, make sure it is done properly and pack and transport the fish or shellfish in ice.
4. With many kinds of fish, and even more so with shellfish and crustaceans, overcooking is a cardinal sin.

Enjoy these dishes and the full measure of culinary pleasure they promise. Whether you are a sport fisherman, recreational shrimper, casual clam digger or simply someone who samples the sea through the medium of grocery shelves, you are in for a delightful and diverse batch of delicacies in the pages that follow. Savor them at your family table or with friends—and bon appetit!

Fish Stock

Ingredients

1 tbsp	butter **or** oil	15 ml
1 3/4 lb	bones and trimmings of white-fleshed fish	790 g
1	onion, chopped	1
1	leek, white part, thinly sliced	1
2	stalks celery, thinly sliced	2
2	shallots, chopped	2
1 1/2 cups	sliced mushrooms	375 ml
1/2 cup	white wine	125 ml
1	lemon, sliced	1
4 cups	water	1 l
1/4 tsp	thyme	1 ml
1	bay leaf	1
10	peppercorns	10
1	bunch parsley	1

Method

1. In a large saucepan, melt the butter and cook the bones and trimmings for 5 minutes.
2. Add the vegetables and continue cooking for another 5 minutes.
3. Deglaze with the wine. Bring to a boil and reduce by half.
4. Add the remaining ingredients and simmer for 25 minutes over low heat.
5. Pour through a strainer and use the stock in fish-based recipes.

Note:

For stronger flavor, add shellfish shells to the fish bones and trimmings, or replace completely to make a seafood stock.

Saltwater Fish

This section of the cookbook covers a considerable variety of saltwater fish species many of which vary dramatically. There's the delicate promise of flatfish such as flounder and halibut, species that appear unsavory but taste wonderful; the rich, oily flavors of the mackerel family; mahi-mahi, dorado and halibut, popular fish commonly found on restaurant menus; the versatile goodness and marvelous flavor afforded by salmon; and the culinary joys of tuna. Saltwater species range from shallow water or inshore fish such as flounder and spot to those found at great depths or far from land.

Saltwater fish can be prepared in many fashions. Here you will find examples of all of the favored approaches—dry cooking (baking, broiling and grilling), wet cooking (poaching, steaming and braising), frying and sautéing. Always remember that, whatever the cooking method of choice, cook quickly and don't overcook. When fish flakes easily but still retains its moisture and has changed from translucent to solid color, it has cooked long enough.

A few keys to selecting saltwater fish, since many of us obtain them from the market as opposed to the old-fashioned means of catching your own, might be helpful. Of course, those fortunate enough to be able to participate in saltwater fishing have no problems with freshness, since they have full control over the care of their catch. There's nothing quite like a meal of fish you have personally caught, and it seems appropriate to note that an old adage suggests that days spent fishing are not counted against one's allotted time on earth.

For those who don't have the opportunity to fish, always remember that good texture and fine flavor derive from freshness. Determining freshness involves smell, looks and feel. Whole fish should have bright pink gills, shiny scales or skin and clear eyes. Fillets, steaks or other cuts should be even-textured, firm and clean, showing no trace of yellow or brown around the edges. Any fresh fish should have a clean, fresh smell as opposed to a strong, "fishy" odor. Some fish, primarily oily ones such as mackerel or blue fish, should be eaten fresh if possible, and certainly they have a freezer life of no longer than a couple of months. They are best grilled or baked, since they carry enough natural oil to make any further infusion of it inadvisable. When you must buy frozen fish (fresh is always preferable) it should have no frost or freezer burn and have been packaged without any air space. There should be no discoloration. With salmon, the development of fish farm technology usually guarantees freshness, and proper commercial salmon fishing should guarantee careful handling — icing the fish down as soon as they are caught.

With properly handled or packaged fish you can hardly go wrong. When you use fish fingers, fillets or steaks, it is often possible, depending on how they were cooked, to enjoy leftovers in sandwiches, fish dip, soups or chowders. You might keep such considerations in mind while using these pages. Whatever the case, these popular, widespread saltwater species promise fine fare on the table.

Sea Bass Steamed over Exotic Fruit Juice with Yogurt Sauce

Ingredients

Herbed Yogurt:

1 cup	plain yogurt	250 ml
2	green onions, chopped **or**	2
1/4 cup	chopped chives	60 ml
2 tbsp	fresh herbs of your choice (basil, coriander, tarragon, lemon balm, etc.)	30 ml
2 tsp	citrus zest (lime, mandarin, grapefruit, orange, etc.) (optional)	10 ml
	salt and freshly ground pepper to taste	
2 tsp	butter	10 ml
1	shallot, chopped	1
1	citrus fruit of your choice – juice and zest (lime, mandarin, grapefruit, orange, etc.)	1
1 cup	exotic fruit juice(s) of your choice (pineapple, mango, papaya, passion fruit, etc.)	250 ml
1/2 cup	white wine	125 ml
	salt and freshly ground pepper to taste	
4	black sea bass fillets, 1/3 lb (150 g) each	4

Method

1. In a small bowl, combine the yogurt, onions, herbs, citrus zest (if desired), salt and pepper. Refrigerate while preparing the fish.

2. In the lower half of a steamer, melt the butter and cook the shallot until soft but not browned.

3. Deglaze with the fruit juices and wine and reduce by a third.

4. Add the zest and season generously.

5. Place the upper half of the steamer (basket with holes) over the lower half containing the juice mixture. Arrange the fillets skin side down and cover. Cook for 5 to 7 minutes, depending on thickness. Serve immediately with the yogurt sauce and fried plantain.

Sea Bass
with Tarragon Beet Coulis

4 SERVINGS

Ingredients

2 tbsp	butter	30 ml
2	large raw beets, diced	2
1	clove garlic, chopped	1
1	shallot, chopped	1
2 cups	fish stock	500 ml
1/4-1/3 cup	35% cream or thick 15% cream	60-80 ml
1-2 tbsp	fresh tarragon **or**	15-30 ml
1-2 tsp	dried tarragon	5-10 ml
4	sea bass fillets, 1/3 lb (150 g) each **or**	4
4	sea bass steaks	4
2 tbsp	oil	30 ml
	salt and freshly ground pepper to taste	

Method

1. In a saucepan, melt the butter and cook the beets with the garlic and shallot over medium heat for 3 to 5 minutes or until the garlic and shallot begin to brown. Season.

2. Add the fish stock and cook, uncovered, for about 20 minutes until the beets are soft.

3. Purée the mixture in a blender or food processor. Add the cream and tarragon. Correct the seasoning. Keep warm.

4. Preheat the barbecue or heat a skillet over medium-high heat. Brush the fish with oil for grilling or heat the oil in the skillet. Cook the fish 3 to 5 minutes per side. Season.

5. Serve on a bed of puréed celeriac, topped with beet coulis and garnished with a sprig of fresh tarragon.

Creole-Style Sauté

4 SERVINGS

Ingredients

1 1/3 lb	cubed sea bass	600 g
2 tbsp	oil	30 ml
1 tbsp	flour	15 ml
2	cloves garlic, chopped	2
1	onion, chopped	1
2	stalks celery, thinly sliced	2
1	green pepper, diced	1
1 can (19 oz)	diced tomatoes	1 can (540 ml)
	salt and freshly ground pepper to taste	
	hot sauce to taste	

Method

1. Sauté the fish cubes in half the oil over medium-high heat. Remove the fish and set aside.

2. Add the remaining oil to the skillet and add the flour. Cook over medium heat until the flour is lightly browned.

3. Stir in the garlic, onion, celery, green pepper and tomatoes. Cook for 2 to 3 minutes.

4. Place the fish in the sauce, season with salt and pepper and add the hot sauce.

5. Serve over rice or pasta.

Fried Ocean Perch with Sweet-and-Sour Sauce

4 SERVINGS

Ingredients

1 tbsp	oil	15 ml
1 tbsp	chopped fresh ginger	15 ml
1	onion, coarsely diced	1
1-2	cloves garlic, chopped	1-2
1	carrot, thinly sliced	1
1 can (6 1/2 oz)	sliced water chestnuts	1 can (199 ml)
1 cup	snow peas	250 ml
1	red pepper, cut into strips	1
1	stalk celery, thinly sliced	1
2/3 cup	water	160 ml
1-2 tbsp	soy sauce	15-30 ml
3 tbsp	tomato sauce	45 ml
2 tbsp	rice vinegar **or** cider vinegar	30 ml
2 tbsp	sugar **or** honey	30 ml
1 tbsp	cornstarch	15 ml
2.2 lb	whole ocean perch or fillets, scaled	1 kg
1 tbsp	salt	15 ml
1 tbsp	pepper	15 ml
1 tbsp	ground coriander	15 ml
1/3 cup	oil	80 ml
1	egg, beaten	1
1/2 cup	cornmeal	125 ml

Method

1. In a skillet, heat the oil. Over medium heat, cook the ginger, onion, garlic, carrot, water chestnuts, snow peas, red pepper and celery until the vegetables are tender. Remove the vegetables from the skillet.

2. In the same skillet, bring to a boil the water, soy sauce, tomato sauce, vinegar and sugar. In the meantime, dissolve the cornstarch in the water and add to the hot liquid. Simmer until thickened. Add the vegetables and keep warm.

3. Rinse the fish and pat dry with paper towels. Make a few diagonal incisions in each side of the fish (skin side only) and sprinkle with salt, pepper and ground coriander.

4. To fry the fish, heat the oil in a wok or a large skillet. In the meantime, dip the fish into the beaten egg and then in the cornmeal, shaking off any excess. Fry the fish 4 to 5 minutes per side. Drain on paper towels and serve with the sweet-and-sour sauce.

Black Sea Bass with Sesame Sauce

4 SERVINGS

Ingredients

1 tbsp	oil	15 ml
2 tsp	chopped fresh ginger	10 ml
3	green onions, finely chopped	3
1/3 cup	tamari sauce	80 ml
1 tbsp	honey	15 ml
1	lime – juice and zest	1
1 tbsp	toasted sesame oil	15 ml
1/4 cup	fish stock **or** water	60 ml
2 tsp	cornstarch	10 ml
2 tsp	cold water	10 ml
4	sea bass fillets, 1/3 lb (150 g) each	4
2 tbsp	sesame seeds	30 ml
	salt and freshly ground pepper to taste	

Method

1. Preheat the oven to 375°F (190°C).
2. In a saucepan, heat the oil and sauté the ginger and green onions for 2 to 3 minutes.
3. Add the tamari sauce, honey, lime juice and zest, sesame oil and stock. Bring to a boil.
4. Dilute the cornstarch with cold water and stir into the bouillon. Correct the seasoning and cook until thickened.
5. In the meantime, place the sea bass fillets on a nonstick baking sheet, season to taste and cook in the center of the oven for 7 to 10 minutes, depending on the thickness of the fillets.
6. Top with the sauce and sprinkle with sesame seeds.

Mackerel
with Green Apple Chutney

Ingredients

1 tbsp	butter	15 ml
1	shallot, chopped	1
1	clove garlic, chopped	1
2	green apples, diced	2
1/4 cup	white vermouth **or** white wine **or** cider	60 ml
3 tbsp	sugar **or** honey **or** maple syrup	45 ml
4	mackerel fillets, 1/3 lb (150 g) each	4
1/4 cup	flour	60 ml
3 tbsp	oil	45 ml
	salt and freshly ground pepper to taste	

Method

1. In a skillet, melt the butter and sauté the shallot and garlic. Add the diced apples, deglaze with the vermouth and cook for 5 to 6 minutes.

2. Season, add the sugar and reduce until a thick syrup is obtained.

3. In the meantime, flour and season the fish fillets.

4. In a skillet, heat the oil over medium-high heat. Fry the fish 3 to 5 minutes per side. Serve with the hot or cold chutney.

Peppered Mackerel
en Papillote

Method

1. Preheat the oven to 375°F (190°C).
2. Make three incisions in the skin of the fish.
3. Insert a half-slice of lemon in each incision.
4. Combine the salt and peppercorns. Sprinkle on each fish.
5. Place the fish on a sheet of aluminum foil.
6. Drizzle the fish with oil and close the foil to form a packet (papillote). Place on a baking sheet and cook in the center of the oven for 18 to 25 minutes.
7. Serve with sautéed vegetables in season.

Note:

Use sea salt for a more subtle taste. The fish can also be barbecued over medium-high heat.

Ingredients

2 2/3 lb	whole mackerel, scaled	1.2 kg
24	lemon slices, halved	24
2 tbsp	crushed peppercorns (pink or green) **or** Szechuan pepper	30 ml
1 tsp	salt	5 ml
3 tbsp	oil	45 ml

Crispy Fish with Cheese

4 SERVINGS

Ingredients

Celery Relish:

1 tbsp	oil	15 ml
4	stalks celery, thinly sliced	4
1/4 cup	chopped green onion	60 ml
1/4 cup	chopped red pepper	60 ml
1 tbsp	finely chopped fresh parsley	15 ml
3 tbsp	sugar	45 ml
1/4 cup	white wine vinegar **or** cider vinegar	60 ml
1/4 tsp	pickling spices	1 ml
	salt and freshly ground pepper to taste	
4	sole fillets, about 1/3 lb (150 g) each	4
1/3 lb	aged Cheddar, cut into four large sticks	150 g
1/3 cup	flour	80 ml
1	egg, beaten	1
1 cup	breadcrumbs	250 ml
	salt and freshly ground pepper to taste	
	oil for frying	

Method

1. In a saucepan, heat the oil and sauté the vegetables. Add the parsley, sugar, vinegar and pickling spices. Season with salt and pepper. Cook until reduced and thickened. Let cool. Refrigerate until ready to serve.

2. Preheat the oven to 375°F (190°C).

3. Place the sole fillets on a work surface and place a stick of cheese at the narrower end of each fillet. Roll the fillets around the cheese sticks.

4. Place the flour in a deep plate and the beaten egg in another. Season the breadcrumbs with the salt and pepper and place in a third plate.

5. Coat the rolled fillets by dredging them in the flour (shaking off any excess), dipping them in the beaten egg and then rolling them in the breadcrumbs. Dip in the egg a second time and roll in the breadcrumbs again.

6. Heat the oil over medium heat and brown the fish fillets on both sides. Place in the oven for 10 to 12 minutes.

7. Serve the fish with the celery relish, either warm or cold.

Flounder Stuffed with Spinach and Dried Tomatoes

Method

1. Preheat the oven to 375°F (190°C).

2. In a food processor, chop 7 oz (200 g) flounder with the tomatoes and shallot. Season.

3. Slice open the flounder fillets horizontally. Stuff with the basil leaves. Add the dried tomato stuffing. Fold over to close and fasten with toothpicks. Place in an oiled ovenproof dish.

4. Bake in the center of the oven for 15 to 20 minutes. Serve immediately, topped with your favorite sauce.

Ingredients

1 1/3 lb	fresh flounder fillets	600 g
8	dried tomatoes, rehydrated	8
1	shallot, finely chopped	1
1/2 cup	fresh basil leaves	125 ml
2 tbsp	olive oil	30 ml
	salt and freshly ground pepper to taste	

Two-Fish Lasagna

6 SERVINGS

Ingredients

1 tbsp	butter	15 ml
1/4 cup	chopped shallot	60 ml
1/2 cup	white wine	125 ml
1 cup	35% cream	250 ml
16	spinach lasagna noodles, cooked	16
1/2 lb	white-fleshed fish fillets	225 g
1/2 cup	chopped rehydrated dried tomatoes	125 ml
1/2 lb	salmon cutlets	225 g
1 1/2 cups	grated cheese of your choice (provolone, mozzarella, Cheddar, Swiss, Friulano, etc.)	375 ml

Method

1. In a saucepan, melt the butter over medium-high heat and sauté the shallot for 5 minutes.

2. Deglaze with the wine and reduce by half.

3. Stir in the cream and simmer until smooth. Season to taste. Set aside.

4. Preheat the oven to 375°F (190°C).

5. Spread some sauce in the bottom of a lasagna dish. Cover with a layer of pasta.

6. Cover the pasta with the white fish fillets and top with another layer of pasta.

7. Cover the pasta with the sauce, spread the chopped tomatoes over top and add another layer of pasta.

8. Top the pasta with the salmon cutlets and add another layer of pasta.

9. Top with sauce and sprinkle with cheese. Bake in the center of the oven for 35 to 45 minutes, until the cheese is toasted.

Bluefin Tuna Tataki
with Asparagus

4 SERVINGS

Method

1. Using a knife or a chopstick, pierce a hole lengthwise through the tuna cubes.
2. Insert the asparagus stalks so that the tips protrude.
3. Roll the tuna cubes in the sesame seeds.
4. In a large skillet, heat the oil over high heat and sear the cubes 1 minute per side.
5. Season to taste and cut the cubes into slices. Serve immediately with herbed garlic mashed potatoes.

Ingredients

1 1/3 lb	bluefin tuna, cut into 2 x 2 x 3-in. (5 x 5 x 7.5-cm) cubes	600 g
8	stalks green asparagus, blanched	8
3 tbsp	sesame seeds	45 ml
2 tbsp	oil	30 ml
	salt and freshly ground pepper to taste	

Tuna Brochettes
with Lemon Grass

4 SERVINGS

Ingredients

Marinade:

1	stalk lemon grass	**1**
1	clove garlic, peeled	**1**
1-2 tsp	chopped fresh ginger	**5-10 ml**
3 tbsp	rice vinegar **or** lemon juice	**45 ml**
1/2 cup	oil	**125 ml**
	a few drops of hot sauce (optional)	
1/4 cup	soy sauce	**60 ml**
	freshly ground pepper to taste	
1 1/3 lb	tuna cubes, about 1 x 1 in. (2.5 x 2.5 cm)	**600 g**
4	green onions, cut into 1-in. (2.5-cm) lengths	**4**

Method

1. Thinly slice the lighter-colored stalk of the lemon grass and place in a food processor. Add the garlic and ginger. Chop finely.

2. Add the vinegar, oil, hot sauce (if desired) and soy sauce. Season with pepper and stir well. Pour the marinade into a shallow dish.

3. Thread the tuna cubes onto the skewers, alternating with the green onion pieces.

4. Place in the marinade and marinate for at least 15 to 30 minutes or up to 2 hours. Cook on a hot grill for 7 to 10 minutes.

Tuna Steaks
with Orange Slices and Almonds

4 SERVINGS

Ingredients

4	tuna steaks, at least 1/3 lb (150 g) each	4
1/3 cup	oil	80 ml
1	orange – zest and slices	1

Vinaigrette:

1	egg yolk	1
1 tbsp	Dijon mustard	15 ml
3/4 cup	oil	180 ml
1/3 cup	orange juice	80 ml
	salt and freshly ground pepper to taste	
6 cups	mixed salad greens	1.5 l
1/2 cup	toasted almonds	125 ml

Method

1. Brush the tuna steaks with oil and sprinkle with orange zest. Let stand for 30 minutes to 1 hour.

2. Prepare the vinaigrette using the same technique as for mayonnaise, by first combining the egg yolk with the mustard and then adding the oil in a thin stream, whisking constantly. Add the orange juice, salt and pepper last.

3. Preheat the barbecue or a skillet over high heat.

4. Arrange the greens on dinner plates. Add the orange slices and sprinkle with the almonds.

5. Drain off any excess oil, season the tuna and cook 3 to 4 minutes per side.

6. Drizzle the vinaigrette over the salad greens and place the tuna steaks on top. Serve immediately.

Bluefin Tuna Carpaccio

M e t h o d

1. Arrange the tuna slices on four individual plates.

2. Arrange the greens in the center.

3. In a bowl, combine the oil and vinegar. Season to taste. Divide among the four plates.

4. Garnish with the Parmesan shavings and season with salt and pepper to taste. Serve immediately.

I n g r e d i e n t s

1 lb	very thinly sliced bluefin tuna	450 g
	salad greens of your choice	
1/4 cup	olive oil	60 ml
2 tbsp	balsamic vinegar	30 ml
2 tbsp	chopped fresh basil	30 ml
3 tbsp	fresh Parmesan shavings	45 ml
	salt and freshly ground pepper to taste	

Mahi Mahi Peanut Satay

4 SERVINGS

Method

1. In a bowl, whisk together all the marinade ingredients until smooth.

2. Add the mahi mahi strips. Coat well, cover and place in the refrigerator to marinate for 20 to 25 minutes.

3. In the meantime, soak bamboo or wood skewers in water.

4. Preheat the grill to medium-hot.

5. Remove the mahi mahi strips from the marinade and thread onto the skewers to make satays.

6. Cook for 5 to 7 minutes, turning only once. Serve immediately, accompanied with your favorite garnish.

Ingredients

Marinade:

3 tbsp	crunchy peanut butter	45 ml
2 tbsp	lemon juice	30 ml
2 tbsp	soy **or** tamari sauce	30 ml
1 tbsp	brown sugar	15 ml
1 tsp	chopped fresh ginger	5 ml
1	clove garlic, finely chopped	1
	crushed chili pepper to taste	
2 tbsp	water	30 ml
1 lb	mahi mahi fillets, cut into strips	450 g

Grilled Mahi Mahi with Orange-Caper Hollandaise Sauce

4 SERVINGS

Ingredients

4	mahi mahi fillets, 1/3 lb (150 g) each	4
1 cup	homemade or store-bought hollandaise sauce	250 ml
1	orange – zest and juice	1
2-3 tbsp	chopped drained capers	30-45 ml
	salt and freshly ground pepper to taste	

Hollandaise Sauce:

1/2 lb	salted butter	252 g
3	egg yolks	3
3 tbsp	orange juice	45 ml
1/2	orange –zest	1/2
	cayenne to taste	
2 tbsp	chopped capers	30 ml
	salt and freshly ground pepper to taste	

Method

1. Cut four large squares each of aluminum foil and parchment paper. Place the parchment on top of the foil. Place a fillet of mahi mahi in the center of each square and season. Fold the foil to make little packets (papillotes).

2. Cook for 7 to 10 minutes on a preheated grill at medium-high heat or in a preheated oven at 425°F (220°C).

3. In the meantime, heat the hollandaise sauce in a saucepan. Stir in the orange juice, half the orange zest and the capers. Cook over low heat for another 1 to 2 minutes, stirring often.

4. Remove the mahi mahi from the foil packets. Top with the orange-caper hollandaise sauce and garnish with the remaining zest. Serve immediately with rice and grilled vegetables.

Note:

Foil packets are a practical way to cook fragile foods on the barbecue or to give them a particular flavor. Parchment paper is added to the foil to prevent the food from sticking.

Hollandaise Sauce:

1. Melt the butter in a double boiler or in the microwave. Clarify by skimming off any foam that forms on the surface. Remove the oil, taking care to leave the whey on the bottom. Set the oil aside.

2. In the top part of the double boiler, vigorously whip the egg yolks. Stir in the orange juice. The water in the bottom part must not touch the bottom of the top part and must never be allowed to boil. Whip until the egg yolks are light and well creamed.

3. Add the butter oil in a thin stream (same procedure as for mayonnaise).

4. Season with the cayenne and add the capers. Correct the seasoning if necessary.

5. Serve immediately over the salmon.

Sea Bream
with Mushroom Stuffing

4 SERVINGS

Ingredients

1	onion, thinly sliced	1
1	clove garlic, chopped	1
2 tbsp	butter	30 ml
3 cups	sliced mushrooms	750 ml
1/3 cup	cognac **or** brandy	80 ml
1/2 tsp	dried thyme	2 ml
1/4 tsp	cayenne	1 ml
1/4 cup	breadcrumbs	60 ml
1/4 cup	grated Parmesan cheese	60 ml
	salt and freshly ground pepper to taste	
8	sea bream fillets 3 oz (75 g) each	8

Method

1. Preheat the grill or oven to 350°F (180°C).

2. In a skillet, sauté the onion and garlic in butter for 2 to 3 minutes.

3. Add the mushrooms and continue cooking for another 5 minutes.

4. Deglaze with the cognac and flambé.

5. Add the thyme, cayenne and breadcrumbs. Cook until all liquid has evaporated.

6. Stir in the Parmesan, season to taste and let cool for 10 minutes.

7. Overlay two fish fillets and stuff them with one-quarter of the mixture. Close the fillets with toothpicks or thread.

8. Place in a buttered ovenproof dish and cook for 10 to 12 minutes in the center of the oven. Serve immediately, accompanied with vegetables in season.

Two-Salmon Tartare

Ingredients

1/2 lb	fresh salmon	225 g
3 oz	smoked salmon	80 g
1	shallot, finely chopped	1
2 tbsp	chopped fresh herbs (chives, chervil, dill, etc.)	30 ml
1 tbsp	chopped capers	15 ml
1	lemon – juice	1
1/4 cup	olive oil	60 ml
4	sprigs fresh herb of your choice	4
	salt and freshly ground pepper to taste	

Method

1. On a work surface, chop the salmon with a knife. Place in a bowl.

2. Add the remaining ingredients and mix well. Let stand for a few minutes and season to taste.

3. Arrange the salmon tartare on four plates and garnish with a sprig of herb. Serve immediately with crackers and rye bread.

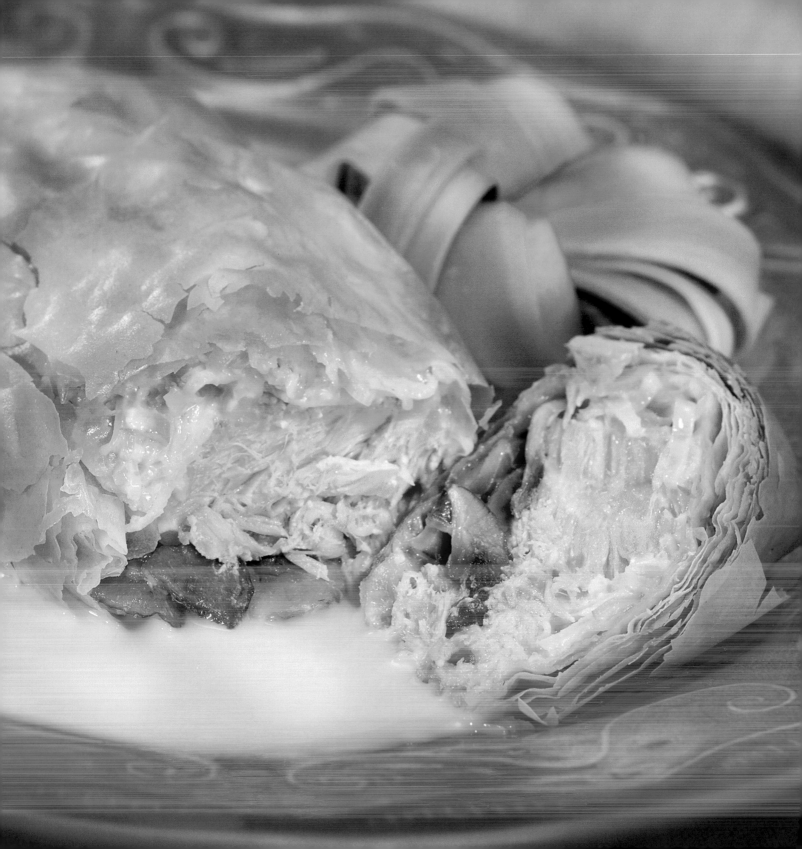

Salmon in Puff Pastry

Ingredients

3 tbsp	oil	45 ml
2 cups	sliced mushrooms	500 ml
2	leeks, white part, thinly sliced	2
1 cup	35% cream	250 ml
1 package (1/2 lb)	store-bought puff pastry dough, thawed	1 package (225 g)
1 1/2 lb	skinned salmon fillet	675 g
	salt and freshly ground pepper to taste	

Method

1. In a skillet, heat 2 tbsp (30 ml) oil and sauté the mushrooms. Season and set aside.

2. In the same skillet, heat the remaining oil and sauté the leeks over medium heat, without browning them.

3. Stir in the cream and reduce by half. Season and set aside.

4. Place the mushrooms on the pastry square, taking care to drain them well.

5. Place the salmon fillet on top of the mushrooms. Season and add the leeks.

6. Brush the edges of the pastry square with the beaten egg.

7. Roll out the remaining dough into a square large enough to cover the salmon. Seal well by pressing the edges together. Baste with the beaten egg and refrigerate for 20 to 45 minutes.

8. Bake in the center of a preheated oven at 400°F (200°C) until the pastry is golden. Serve alone or with your favorite sauce.

Note:

The mushrooms may be replaced with spinach and citrus zest, and fresh or dried herbs may be added to the leek mixture.

Salmon Burgers

Ingredients

1 lb	chopped salmon	450 g
1 tbsp	chopped capers	15 ml
1 tsp	Dijon mustard	5 ml
1/2 tsp	crushed coriander seeds	2 ml
2 tbsp	chopped green onion	30 ml
2 tbsp	grated Parmesan	30 ml
	salt and freshly ground pepper to taste	
4	hamburger buns	4

Method

1. Preheat the grill or the oven to 425°F (220°C).

2. In a bowl, combine all the ingredients except the buns. Season to taste.

3. Divide the mixture into four patties.

4. Place on a grill or baking sheet in the center of the oven and cook for 10 to 15 minutes, turning them only once.

5. Heat the buns and serve the burgers with your favorite toppings.

Note:

The burgers can also be fried in a skillet over medium-high heat.

Salmon
with Wasabi Butter

Method

1. Prepare the wasabi butter by combining the wasabi with the water. Stir until smooth. Add the butter and the chives. Set aside.

2. Preheat the oven to 425°F (220°C).

3. Place the salmon fillets on a baking sheet. Season and cook in the center of the oven for 7 to 12 minutes, depending on the thickness of the fillets and desired degree of doneness.

4. Serve the salmon with a knob of wasabi butter and a lemon quarter, accompanied with sautéed vegetables and sticky rice.

Ingredients

1 tbsp	wasabi powder	15 ml
1 tbsp	water	15 ml
3 tbsp	softened butter	45 ml
2 tbsp	chopped chives	30 ml
4	salmon fillets, about 1/3 lb (150 g) each	4
	salt and freshly ground pepper to taste	

Halibut Roll-Ups with Tapenade

4 SERVINGS

Ingredients

Tapenade:

1	clove garlic, green center removed	1
1/2 cup	pitted black **or** green olives	125 ml
1/3 cup	olive oil	80 ml
	salt and freshly ground pepper to taste	
1 1/3 lb	halibut fillet	600 g

Method

1. Preheat the oven to 400°F (200°C).

2. To make the tapenade, process the garlic and the olives in a food processor until finely ground.

3. Add the oil (reserving 1 tbsp [15 ml]) and mix well until smooth. Season to taste.

4. Cut the halibut fillet into 4 long strips. Brush the strips with the tapenade on one side only.

5. Roll the strips so that the tapenade is on the inside and use toothpicks or thread to hold the roll-ups together.

6. Place the roll-ups in an ovenproof dish and brush the tops with the remaining olive oil.

7. Bake in the oven for 10 to 12 minutes. Remove the thread or toothpicks and serve the roll-ups with colorful vegetables.

Halibut with Sorrel

Ingredients

4	halibut fillets, about 1/3 lb (150 g) each	4
1 tbsp	melted butter	15 ml
1 tbsp	butter	15 ml
1	shallot, chopped	1
1/2 cup	white wine	125 ml
1/2 cup	35% cream	125 ml
1/2 lb	fresh sorrel, washed and stemmed	225 g
	salt and freshly ground pepper to taste	

Method

1. Preheat the oven to 400°F (200°C).

2. Place the halibut fillets, skin side down, on a baking sheet. Brush with butter and season. Cook in the center of the oven for 7 to 12 minutes, depending on the thickness of the fillets and the desired degree of doneness.

3. In the meantime, heat the butter in a skillet and cook the shallot over medium heat.

4. Deglaze the skillet with the white wine and reduce by half.

5. Stir in the cream, bring to a boil and simmer for 3 to 4 minutes. Season. Place the fillets on a bed of sorrel and top with the cream sauce. Serve with rice, pasta or potatoes and your favorite vegetables.

Halibut Fish and Chips

Method

1. In a large bowl, beat the egg and stir in one-third of the flour.

2. Add one-third of the beer. Continue adding the flour and beer alternately. Season and refrigerate for 1 hour.

3. Pat the fish fillets dry with paper towels.

4. Dip the fillets in the batter.

5. Heat the oil and, when hot, add the fish fillets. Fry until golden. Place on paper towels. Serve immediately with homemade French fries and tartar sauce.

Variation:

Add 2 tbsp (30 ml) unsweetened grated coconut to the batter.

Ingredients

1	egg	1
2 1/4 cups	pastry flour	560 ml
1 cup	beer **or** milk	250 ml
	salt and freshly ground pepper to taste	
1 1/3 lb	halibut fillets	600 g
	canola oil	

Halibut with Tomatoes au Gratin

Ingredients

1 tbsp	oil	15 ml
1	onion, chopped	1
1/2 cup	white wine	125 ml
1 can (19 oz)	diced tomatoes	1 can (540 ml)
1	bay leaf	1
1	sprig fresh thyme **or**	1
1/2 tsp	dried thyme	2 ml
3 tbsp	oil	45 ml
4	cloves garlic, chopped	4
1 1/3 lb	halibut fillet	600 g
2/3 lb	sliced or grated cheese of your choice (Swiss, Cheddar, mozzarella, provolone, etc.)	300 g
	salt and freshly ground pepper to taste	

Method

1. In a saucepan, heat the oil and cook the onion for 2 to 3 minutes.
2. Deglaze with the wine and reduce by one-third.
3. Add the tomatoes, bay leaf and thyme. Simmer for 15 to 20 minutes or until the sauce has thickened. Season to taste.
4. In the meantime, in a skillet, heat the oil over medium heat and cook the garlic until soft and golden, about 10 minutes. Remove the garlic and add it to the tomato mixture.
5. Increase the heat to high and quickly sear the halibut, 2 to 3 minutes per side. Season.
6. Divide the fish among four small au gratin dishes or place in a large au gratin dish. Top with the tomato mixture, cover with cheese and place in the oven until the cheese is toasted.
7. Serve with fresh pasta and green vegetables.

Bonito Teriyaki

Ingredients

Marinade:

1	clove garlic, chopped	1
1 tbsp	chopped fresh ginger	15 ml
1/3 cup	rice wine (mirin) **or** sherry	80 ml
1/3 cup	soy sauce	80 ml
2 tbsp	sugar	30 ml
1 tbsp	oil	15 ml
1 1/3 lb	bonito fillets or steaks	600 g

Method

1. Combine all the marinade ingredients. Pour into a shallow dish.
2. Place the fish in the marinade and marinate for at least 30 minutes and no more than 4 hours.
3. Drain the fish and pour the marinade into a small saucepan.
4. Boil the marinade for 5 minutes and use it for basting the fish while it cooks.
5. Cook the fish on the hot grill or in a preheated oven at 400°F (200°C) for 7 to 10 minutes.

Fish and Seafood Brochettes with Pineapple Curry

4 SERVINGS

Ingredients

4	large scallops	4
4	large raw shrimp, peeled	4
16	1-in. (2.5-cm) cubes grouper	16
8	chunks zucchini	8
4	cherry tomatoes	4
4	shallots, peeled	4
1/3 cup	oil	80 ml
2 tbsp	curry paste of your choice	30 ml
1 cup	pineapple juice	250 ml
2	green onions, sliced	2
1	clove garlic, chopped	1
1 tbsp	honey	15 ml

Method

1. Thread the following onto four 10-in. (25-cm) skewers: a chunk of zucchini, two cubes of each fish, a scallop, a shrimp, a chunk of zucchini, two cubes of fish and a cherry tomato. Place in a shallow dish.

2. Combine the remaining ingredients and pour over the brochettes. Marinate in the refrigerator for at least 1 hour.

3. Preheat the grill to medium hot.

4. Drain the brochettes, saving the marinade.

5. Grill the brochettes 2 to 3 minutes per side, basting with the marinade, until the scallops are opaque and the shrimp are pink.

Fish Ravioli

Ingredients

1 tbsp	sesame oil	15 ml
1	clove garlic, chopped	1
1/2	onion, chopped	1/2
1/4 cup	thinly sliced shiitake mushrooms	60 ml
1/2 cup	chopped napa **or** Chinese cabbage	125 ml
1/3 cup	grated carrot	80 ml
2 tsp	chopped fresh ginger	10 ml
1 tbsp	soy sauce	15 ml
	pinch of Chinese five-spice powder	
1 tbsp	fish sauce	15 ml
	freshly ground pepper to taste	
1/2 lb	chopped fresh fish	225 g
40	wonton wrappers	40
1	egg, beaten	1

Coriander Butter:

1/2 cup	melted butter	125 ml
1/2 cup	chopped fresh coriander	125 ml
	salt and freshly ground pepper to taste	

Method

1. Heat the sesame oil in a skillet and sauté the garlic, onions, mushrooms, napa cabbage and carrot.

2. Add the ginger, soy sauce, Chinese five-spice, fish sauce and pepper. Cook for 2 minutes and remove from heat. Let cool and add the fish.

3. In the meantime, bring 16 to 20 cups (4 to 5 liters) of salted water to a boil.

4. Place 20 wonton wrappers on a work surface. Brush the edges of each one with the beaten egg. Place 1 to 2 tbsp (15 to 30 ml) of fish filling in the center of each wrapper. Cover with a second wrapper and press firmly around the edges to seal.

5. Boil the ravioli in the boiling water for 7 to 10 minutes.

6. Drain and serve with hot coriander butter.

Coriander Butter

1. Combine all the ingredients.

2. Reheat in the microwave or on the stovetop just before serving.

Fish Loaf
with Cheese and Vegetables

Method

1. In a skillet, heat the oil and sauté the onion and garlic.

2. Add the zucchini, broccoli, cauliflower and red pepper. Cook until tender.

3. Add the paprika and thyme. Season generously with salt and pepper.

4. Place the mixture in a food processor and process until finely chopped. Add the remaining ingredients.

5. Pour into a large, greased loaf pan and bake in a preheated oven at 375°F (190°C) for 25 to 30 minutes. Serve with homemade ketchup.

Ingredients

2 tbsp	oil	30 ml
1	onion, chopped	1
2	cloves garlic, chopped	2
1/2	zucchini, diced	1/2
1/2 cup	broccoli florets	125 ml
1/2 cup	cauliflower florets	125 ml
1/2 cup	thinly sliced red pepper	125 ml
2 tsp	paprika	10 ml
1-2 tbsp	fresh thyme	15-30 ml
2	potatoes, cooked and cut into pieces	2
2	eggs	2
1 lb	chopped raw fish of your choice	450 g
1/3 cup	35% cream	80 ml
1/2 cup	breadcrumbs	125 ml
3 tbsp	tomato paste	45 ml
2/3 cup	grated Parmesan	160 ml
1/3 cup	grated cheese of your choice (Gouda, Swiss, Cheddar, etc.)	80 ml
	salt and freshly ground pepper to taste	

Shellfish and Crustaceans

In many locations in North America, and indeed across the world, finding evidence of man's long-established love affair with shellfish and crustaceans poses no problem. In estuaries and along tidal creeks and rivers, in back bays and countless marshes, a traveler encounters constant reminders of man's reliance on shellfish and crustaceans for sustenance and dining pleasure. Vast middens, immense heaps of discarded oyster and clamshells, reveal the presence of prehistoric settlements. Piles of oyster shells surrounding quaint little seafood restaurants or fish camps in out-of-the-way locations offer mute testimony to past and present culinary joys. There are endless miles of back roads surfaced with crushed shells. You can rest assured that before those shells ever began to serve this mundane purpose they yielded the source of mouthwatering feasts.

Crustaceans and shellfish, it must be admitted, may at first seem unappealing to the eye. Yet inside forms only a mother could love are hidden incredible delicacies. As with fish, freshness is vital. Lobsters, oysters, crabs, clams and mussels should ideally be alive when purchased. Fresh shellfish should convey the odor of a refreshing sea breeze, and clams, mussels and oysters, shells that are open prior to cooking should be treated with suspicion. Tap them lightly and if they do not close discard them. Scallops, whether of the bay, calico or sea variety, should be creamy white in color, although they will occasionally show some hints of pink or tan. The liquid of shucked oysters should be milky or light gray in appearance while the actual oysters should appear creamy white. Shrimp should have a mild odor and feel firm to the touch—any shrimp that is soft or "squishy" needs to be discarded. Finally, be certain that any

shellfish you personally harvest come from clean, unpolluted waters. When an area has been closed to shellfishing, that step has been taken for good reasons.

Store all shellfish as close to freezing temperatures (33-34 degrees Fahrenheit or 1-2 degrees Centigrade) as possible when refrigerating them, and remember that they have a short shelf life. No matter what type of shellfish or crustaceans you use, clean them thoroughly prior to cooking. For live crabs or lobsters this involves nothing more than a good rinsing before introducing them to boiling water, but oysters, clams and mussels should be scrubbed briskly. With clams repeated soakings in salt water encourages them to spit out grit, while soaking mussels in cold water will loosen sand and reduce what can be an overly salty flavor.

As with fish, overcooking shellfish and crustaceans is a cardinal sin. Oysters that have been roasted or steamed too long become rubbery, overcooked shrimp and lobsters become tough, as do crabs and scallops. That may not be a major factor in some of these recipes, but in every case adhere closely to the instructions on heat and time. Also keep in mind the fact that with oysters they are delicious eaten raw.

Whatever approach you try with the shellfish and crustacean recipes offered here, many would argue that there's no fining eating. A two-pound lobster seems to disappear as if by magic, and a mountain of shrimp or oysters turns out to be little more than a hearty serving for a hungry soul. From the simple to the complex, these wonders of the coastline tempt us with tastes that carry one close to the culinary realms of the gods.

Lobster in Court Bouillon

Ingredients

Court Bouillon:

1	carrot, peeled and sliced	1
1	stalk celery, cut into pieces	1
1	onion, coarsely chopped	1
8 cups	water	2 l
1	lemon – juice	1
2 tbsp	white vinegar **or** cider vinegar	30 ml
1	bay leaf	1
5-10	peppercorns	5-10
1 tbsp	coarse salt	15 ml
1/2 tsp	dried thyme	2 ml
4	live lobsters, 1 lb (450 g) each	4

Method

1. In a large saucepan, combine all the ingredients for the court bouillon. Bring to a boil and simmer for 20 minutes.

2. Bring to a boil again and plunge the lobsters into the court bouillon, head first. Boil for 12 to 15 minutes. Serve immediately with melted butter and your favorite side dish.

Lobster with Vanilla Butter

4 SERVINGS

M e t h o d

1. In a small saucepan, melt the butter with the shallot and vanilla pod over low heat until the butter is hot.
2. Season with pepper to taste and add the parsley. Keep warm for 10 minutes.
3. Remove the vanilla pod and serve the lobster with your favorite side dishes.

I n g r e d i e n t s

1/2 cup	salted butter	125 ml
1	shallot, chopped	1
1	vanilla pod, scraped and split in two	1
	freshly ground pepper to taste	
2 tbsp	chopped fresh parsley	30 ml
4	warm lobsters, 1 1/2 lb (675 g) each, cooked in court bouillon	4

Lobster with Herbed Oil

4 SERVINGS

Ingredients

3/4 cup	olive oil	180 ml
1/3 cup	chopped fresh herbs of your choice (parsley, dill, chives, tarragon, basil, etc.)	80 ml
1 tbsp	lemon juice	15 ml
	salt and freshly ground pepper to taste	
4	warm lobsters, cooked in court bouillon	4

Method

1. In a small saucepan, heat the oil for 2 minutes over high heat. Remove the saucepan from the heat.

2. Add the herbs and stir well. Let cool.

3. Stir in the lemon juice and season to taste.

4. Shell the lobsters. Drizzle with herbed oil and serve immediately with a vegetable risotto.

Lobster Salad
with Ginger and Tarragon

Method

1. Cut the lobsters into pieces and set aside.

2. In a small saucepan, cook the shallot and ginger in the oil for 2 minutes. Let cool.

3. Stir in the honey, vinegar and tarragon. Season to taste.

4. Serve the lobster on a bed of greens, topped with the vinaigrette.

Ingredients

4	lobsters, cooked in court bouillon and shelled	4
2 tbsp	chopped shallot	30 ml
1 tbsp	chopped fresh ginger	15 ml
1/4 cup	olive oil	60 ml
1 tbsp	honey	15 ml
2 tbsp	red wine vinegar	30 ml
2 tbsp	chopped fresh tarragon	30 ml
	salt and freshly ground pepper to taste	
	mixed baby greens	

Vodka Oyster Shooters

Ingredients

4	fresh oysters	4
1/4 cup	chilled vodka	60 ml
12	pink peppercorns	12
4	coriander leaves	4

Method

1. Using a brush, thoroughly scrub the oysters under cold water, without submerging them.
2. Open the oyster shells and place one oyster in each shooter glass.
3. Pour 1 tbsp (15 ml) vodka over each oyster.
4. Add three pink peppercorns and a coriander leaf to each glass. Serve immediately.

Note:

If you don't have shooter glasses, you can serve the oysters in Asian soup spoons.

Ginger Sesame Oysters

4 SERVINGS

Ingredients

24	fresh oysters	24
1	lime – zest and juice	1
1 tsp	toasted sesame oil	5 ml
1 tsp	finely chopped fresh ginger	5 ml
1 tbsp	finely diced red pepper	15 ml
1 tsp	plain or toasted sesame seeds	5 ml
	hot sauce to taste	

Method

1. Using a brush, thoroughly scrub the oysters under cold water, without submerging them.

2. Open the oysters and place them on a serving platter covered with coarse salt to keep them from slipping.

3. Garnish with the remaining ingredients and serve immediately on their own or with a salad.

Note:

Pickled ginger can be substituted for fresh ginger.

Oysters au Gratin

Ingredients

Mornay Sauce:

1 tbsp	butter	15 ml
1 tbsp	flour	15 ml
3/4 cup	hot milk	180 ml
	pinch of ground nutmeg	
	salt and freshly ground pepper to taste	
1/2 cup	grated Swiss cheese	125 ml
24	fresh oysters	24
2 tbsp	chopped fresh parsley	30 ml

Method

1. In a saucepan, melt the butter over medium heat. Add the flour and stir to make a roux. Continue cooking without letting the mixture brown.

2. Gradually whisk in the hot milk. Add the nutmeg, bring to a boil and simmer gently until the desired thickness is obtained.

3. In the meantime, using a brush, thoroughly scrub the oysters under cold water, without submerging them. Open the oyster shells and place the oysters on a baking sheet sprinkled with coarse salt to keep them from slipping.

4. Season the sauce and stir in the cheese until it melts.

5. Top the oysters with the sauce, sprinkle with parsley and place under the broiler in a preheated oven. Serve as a first course (six oysters per person).

Smoked Oysters

MAKES 36

I n g r e d i e n t s

36	fresh oysters	36
	Seasonings:	
2 tbsp	fresh herbs (rosemary, basil, thyme, etc.) **or**	30 ml
2 tsp	dried herbs	10 ml
	freshly ground pepper to taste	
3 cups	untreated wood chips (maple, cherry, hickory, etc.)	750 ml

M e t h o d

1. Open the oysters, drain, dry with paper towels and set aside.

2. In a shallow dish, combine all the seasonings.

3. Place the oysters in the dish and coat well with the seasonings. Cover and refrigerate for about 2 hours.

4. Soak the wood chips in cold water for 30 minutes to 1 hour.

5. Drain the wood chips and wrap in aluminum foil. Prick a few holes in the foil.

6. Place the wood chips on the barbecue grill and heat over medium-high heat for 7 to 8 minutes or until they begin to smolder. Turn off one of the burners and turn the other one down to minimum heat.

7. Remove the oysters from the seasonings and place on a rack on a baking sheet. Place the baking sheet on the barbecue grill on the side that has been turned off. Smoke for 30 minutes to 1 hour. Do not let the oysters brown.

8. Let cool to lukewarm and serve on crackers or in a salad.

Saffron Mussels

4 SERVINGS

Ingredients

4.4 lb	cleaned fresh mussels	2 kg
1 tbsp	butter	15 ml
1/4 cup	chopped shallot	60 ml
3/4 cup	white wine	180 ml
1/4 tsp	saffron threads or ground saffron	1 ml
1 cup	35% cream	250 ml
1 tbsp	chopped fresh parsley	15 ml
	salt and freshly ground pepper to taste	

Method

1. Wash the mussels and drain well in a sieve. Set aside.

2. In a large saucepan, melt the butter and cook the shallot over medium heat until soft but not browned.

3. Stir in the white wine and saffron. Reduce by half over medium-high heat.

4. Add the mussels, cover and cook for 8 to 12 minutes, stirring three times.

5. Remove the mussels from the saucepan. Keep warm.

6. Stir the cream into the remaining cooking juices. Reduce until smooth. Add the parsley and season to taste. Serve the mussels topped with the sauce.

Note:

When washing the mussels, check to ensure that they are fresh. Tap any shells that are open and discard the ones that do not close.

Mussel and Grilled Pepper Salad

Ingredients

4.4 lb	washed fresh mussels	2 kg
2	red peppers	2
1	green pepper	1
1	yellow pepper	1
4	green onions, chopped	4
1	clove garlic, chopped	1
1-2 tbsp	drained capers	15-30 ml
1-2 tsp	fresh herbs of your choice (thyme, basil, oregano, parsley, chives, etc.)	5-10 ml
1/4-1/3 cup	olive oil	60-80 ml
2-3 tbsp	cider vinegar	30-45 ml
	salt and freshly ground pepper to taste	

Method

1. In a large pot, bring 2 cups (500 ml) water to boil and cook the mussels until they open. Let cool before shelling.

2. Blacken the peppers in the oven or on the grill. Peel, seed and cut into wide strips. Place in a bowl.

3. Add the onions, garlic, capers, herbs and mussels, and stir.

4. Stir in the oil and vinegar. Season. Serve warm or chilled.

Marinated Mussels

Method

1. In a large pot, melt the butter and sauté the shallots over medium heat for 3 to 4 minutes.

2. Add the parsley, thyme, bay leaf, wine and vinegar. Season with salt and pepper to taste.

3. Increase the heat to high and bring to a boil. Add the mussels, cover and cook until the mussels open. Stir occasionally. Remove the pot from the heat.

4. Arrange the mussels on deep plates. Whisk the second amount of butter into the cooking liquid. Pour over the mussels and sprinkle with parsley.

Ingredients

2 tbsp	butter	30 ml
3	shallots, chopped	3
2 tbsp	chopped fresh parsley	30 ml
1	sprig thyme	1
1	small bay leaf	1
1 cup	white wine	250 ml
1 tbsp	white wine vinegar	15 ml
	salt and freshly ground pepper to taste	
4.4 lb	cleaned fresh mussels	2 kg
2 tbsp	butter	30 ml
2 tbsp	chopped fresh parsley	30 ml

Pasta with Mussels

4 SERVINGS

Ingredients

1 tbsp	oil	15 ml
1/4 cup	chopped onion	60 ml
2	cloves garlic, chopped	2
1/4 cup	minced red pepper	60 ml
1/4 cup	chopped celery	60 ml
1 cup	white wine **or** apple juice	250 ml
4.4 lb	cleaned fresh mussels	2 kg
1 cup	35% cream	250 ml
2	bunches chopped fresh basil	2
1 lb	cooked long pasta of your choice	450 g

Method

1. In a saucepan, heat the oil and sauté the vegetables.
2. Deglaze with the wine and reduce by half.
3. Add the mussels; cover and simmer for 2 minutes or until the mussels open. Remove the mussels. Shell the mussels and discard the shells. Keep warm.
4. Stir the cream into the cooking liquid. Reduce until smooth and creamy. Season to taste.
5. Add the basil, pasta and mussels. Stir well and serve.

Caribbean Rice with Seafood

Ingredients

2 tbsp	oil	30 ml
2	cloves garlic, chopped	2
1	onion, thinly sliced	1
1	plantain, thinly sliced	1
1	red pepper, diced	1
1	stalk lemon grass, cut into 2-in. (5-cm) lengths	1
1 cup	long-grain rice	250 ml
1 2/3 cups	water **or** fish stock	410 ml
2/3 cup	drained and rinsed canned black beans	160 ml
	salt and freshly ground pepper to taste	
1/2 lb	raw shrimp	225 g
2 lb	cleaned fresh clams	900 g

Method

1. In a saucepan, heat the oil and sauté the garlic, onion, plantain and red pepper.

2. Add the lemon grass and rice. Season generously with salt and pepper. Add the stock or water. Bring to a boil, lower the heat, cover and simmer for 15 to 18 minutes.

3. Five minutes before the rice is done, add the black beans, shrimp and clams.

4. Stir well, correct the seasoning and remove the lemon grass. Serve immediately.

Clam Chowder

Ingredients

1 tbsp	oil	15 ml
3	slices bacon, thinly sliced	3
1	onion, chopped	1
1/2 cup	chopped celery	125 ml
1/2 cup	diced carrot	125 ml
1 cup	white wine	250 ml
4 cups	fish stock	1 l
1	bay leaf	1
2 lb	fresh clams	900 g
1 1/2 cups	cubed potatoes	375 ml
1/3 cup	35% cream	80 ml
1	fresh tomato, diced	1
1 tbsp	chopped fresh parsley	15 ml

Method

1. Wash the clams.
2. In a large pot, heat the oil over high heat and sauté the bacon for 2 minutes.
3. Add the vegetables and continue cooking for 5 minutes over medium heat.
4. Add the wine and reduce by half.
5. Add the stock and bay leaf and bring to a boil.
6. Add the clams and continue cooking until they open.
7. Remove the clams, let stand for 5 minutes and shell.
8. Add the potatoes and cook for another 10 to 15 minutes over medium heat.
9. Whisk in the cream and add the clams to reheat. Correct the seasoning.
10. Serve immediately, garnished with the diced tomato and chopped parsley.

Crab and Asparagus Flan

Ingredients

1/2 bunch	fresh asparagus **or**	1/2 bunch
1 can (14 oz)	asparagus	1 can (396 ml)
2	crabs, cooked in court bouillon and shelled	2
1/3 cup	35% cream	80 ml
1/3 cup	milk	80 ml
2	eggs	2
	salt and freshly ground pepper to taste	
	pinch of nutmeg	

Method

1. Preheat the oven to 350°F (180°C).

2. In a saucepan, cook the asparagus (if using fresh) for 5 minutes in boiling water and drain.

3. In the meantime, divide the crabmeat among four buttered ramekins. Place the ramekins in an ovenproof dish.

4. In a food processor, purée the asparagus with the cream until smooth.

5. Add the remaining ingredients; mix well and season. Pour the mixture over the crab. Fill the ovenproof dish with water so it is halfway up the sides of the ramekins. Bake in the center of the oven for 30 to 45 minutes.

6. Serve in the ramekins, garnished with pieces of crabmeat and asparagus tips.

Crab Spring Rolls

Ingredients

4	large sheets rice paper	4
1 cup	cooked rice vermicelli	250 ml
2/3 cup	julienned carrot	160 ml
2/3 cup	julienned cucumber	160 ml
2/3 cup	julienned red pepper	160 ml
2-3	crabs, cooked in court bouillon and shelled	2-3
8	fresh mint leaves	8
2 tbsp	homemade or store-bought mayonnaise	30 ml
2 tsp	lemon zest	10 ml

Method

1. Soak the rice paper in lukewarm water to soften, 10 to 12 seconds. Place on a clean dish towel.

2. Place the rice vermicelli along the bottom third of each sheet. Place the julienned vegetables and crabmeat on top of the vermicelli. Add a mint leaf and a little mayonnaise.

3. Roll up the rice paper around the filling. Refrigerate for at least 30 minutes before serving with your favorite sauce.

Note:

Spring rolls are often served with peanut sauce.

Stuffed Crab

4 SERVINGS

Ingredients

4	live crabs	4
1 cup	soft bread cubes	250 ml
1 cup	milk	250 ml
1 tbsp	oil	15 ml
1 tbsp	butter	15 ml
1	clove garlic, chopped	1
1	onion, chopped	1
3 tbsp	chopped fresh parsley	45 ml
2 tbsp	lemon juice	30 ml
2	tomatoes, diced	2
	salt and freshly ground pepper to taste	
3–4 tbsp	breadcrumbs	45–60 ml
2–3 tbsp	melted butter	30–45 ml

Method

1. Preheat the oven to 425°F (220°C).

2. Cook the crabs using the court bouillon method for lobster on page 71.

3. Let cool until lukewarm before shelling the crabs. Set aside the flesh and clean the shells, which will be used later for serving.

4. In a small bowl, combine the soft bread cubes with the milk. Set aside.

5. In a skillet, heat the oil and melt the butter.

6. Cook the garlic and onion for 3 to 5 minutes, until soft but not browned.

7. Add the parsley, lemon juice and tomatoes. Mix well.

8. Stir in the bread-cube mixture and crabmeat. Season to taste.

9. Fill the crab shells with the mixture and cover with breadcrumbs and melted butter. Bake in the oven until golden. Serve with your favorite vegetables.

Anise-Flavored Shrimp

M e t h o d

1. In a skillet, melt the butter over medium-high heat and cook the shallot and fennel until soft but not browned. Remove and set aside.

2. In the same skillet, sauté the shrimp over high heat until they turn pink. Set aside with the vegetables.

3. Deglaze the skillet with the liqueur.

4. Add the cream and simmer until thickened. Season to taste, add the shrimp to the sauce to reheat and serve immediately.

Note:

This sauce may also be prepared with other types of seafood or fish.

I n g r e d i e n t s

1 tbsp	butter	15 ml
2 tbsp	chopped shallot	30 ml
1/2 cup	julienned fennel bulb	125 ml
1 1/3 lb	peeled raw shrimp	600 g
1/3 cup	anise liqueur (pastis, pernod, sambuca, etc.)	80 ml
1 1/2 cups	35% cream	375 ml
	salt and freshly ground pepper to taste	

Shrimp Bisque

Ingredients

2	carrots, diced	2
1	onion, chopped	1
1/2	fennel bulb, thinly sliced	1/2
2 tbsp	butter	30 ml
2 lb	deveined, peeled raw shrimp	900 g
1 1/2 cups	dry white wine	375 ml
2 cups	fish stock **or** chicken stock	500 ml
1 can (19 oz)	diced Italian tomatoes	1 can (540 ml)
1 tbsp	tomato paste	15 ml
1	bouquet garni	1
1/3 cup	uncooked rice	80 ml
1/3 cup	35% cream	80 ml
	salt and freshly ground pepper to taste	
2 tsp	chopped fresh parsley	10 ml

Method

1. In a large saucepan, cook the vegetables in butter over medium-high heat until soft but not browned.
2. Add the shrimp shells and cook for 2 minutes.
3. Stir in the wine and reduce by half, uncovered.
4. Add the stock, tomatoes, tomato paste and bouquet garni. Simmer for 20 minutes.
5. Strain through a sieve and return the stock to the saucepan. Add the shrimp and cook for 5 to 7 minutes. Remove and set aside.
6. Add the rice to the stock and cook for 15 minutes.
7. Purée in a food processor until smooth. Add the cream and season to taste.
8. Serve hot, sprinkled with chopped parsley.

Note:

Different herbs may be used, and lemon zest may be added.

Shrimp in Jackets
with Spicy Red Pepper Dip

Ingredients

1 1/3 cups	water	330 ml
1/4 cup	Madeira **or** cognac	60 ml
1/2	lemon – zest and juice	1/2
1 lb	peeled raw shrimp	450 g

Dip:

1 tbsp	butter **or** oil	15 ml
1	red pepper, coarsely chopped	1
1/2	onion, coarsely chopped	1/2
1	hot pepper **or** a few drops hot sauce	1
1 tbsp	chopped fresh herbs of your choice (basil, thyme, oregano, coriander, etc.)	15 ml
24	snow peas, blanched	24
	salt and freshly ground pepper to taste	

Method

1. In a saucepan, combine the water, Madeira, lemon juice and zest to make a court bouillon. Bring to a boil and season generously.

2. Cook the shrimp in the court bouillon. When done, remove and cool rapidly without rinsing. Set aside 1/2 cup (125 ml) court bouillon.

3. In the same saucepan, melt the butter and sauté the red pepper and onion.

4. Add the reserved court bouillon, hot pepper or hot sauce and simmer until the pepper is soft.

5. In the meantime, wrap each shrimp in a snow pea and fasten with a toothpick or cocktail pick. Refrigerate.

6. Purée the pepper in a food processor; add the herbs and season. Remove the hot pepper before puréeing if a milder-tasting dip is desired.

7. Chill until serving.

Shrimp-Stuffed Avocados

4 SERVINGS

Ingredients

2	ripe avocados	2
1/3 cup	plain yogurt	80 ml
2 tbsp	orange juice	30 ml
1 tsp	chopped fresh coriander	5 ml
	salt and freshly ground pepper to taste	
1	tomato, finely diced	1
1/2	yellow pepper, finely diced	1/2
2	green onions, chopped	2
1 1/2 cups	peeled cooked shrimp	375 ml

Method

1. Cut the avocados in half, remove the pits, scoop out the flesh and dice finely. Set aside the avocado shells.

2. Place the diced avocado in a bowl and immediately add the yogurt, orange juice and coriander to keep the avocado from darkening. Season generously.

3. Add the vegetables and mix well.

4. Gently stir in the shrimp. Set aside 12 nice shrimp for garnish.

5. Fill the avocado shells with the mixture and garnish with the shrimp.

6. Place on plates. Decorate with orange slices and a sprig of coriander.

Spicy Crêpes with Coconut Shrimp Filling

4 SERVINGS

Ingredients

Crêpe Batter:

1	egg	1
1/2 tbsp	sugar	7 ml
2 tbsp	melted butter, cooled	30 ml
3/4 cup	milk	180 ml
2/3 cup	flour	160 ml
	pinch of ground ginger	
	pinch of ground nutmeg	
	pinch of ground cinnamon	
	pinch of ground cayenne	
	salt and freshly ground pepper to taste	
	oil **or** butter for frying	

Filling:

1 tbsp	oil	15 ml
1 lb	large raw shrimp	450 g
1 cup	snow peas	250 ml
1 cup	julienned carrot	250 ml
4	green onions, chopped	4
1 tsp	finely chopped fresh ginger	5 ml
1-2	cloves garlic, chopped	1-2
1 tsp	curry powder or paste	5 ml
1/2 cup	unsweetened grated coconut	125 ml
1/2	lemon – zest and juice	1/2
1/4 cup	coconut milk **or** 35% cream	60 ml

Method

Crêpe Batter

1. Beat the egg and sugar and gradually whisk in the butter.

2. Stir in the milk, whisking until just blended.

3. In a large bowl, sift the flour with the spices, salt and pepper. Make a well in the center of the flour.

4. Pour the liquid into the well and stir in gradually. Let the batter stand for at least 30 minutes before preparing the crêpes. Makes four large crêpes.

Filling

5. In the meantime, heat the oil in a skillet over high heat and sauté the shrimp with the vegetables, ginger and garlic.

6. Add the curry powder and cook for 2 minutes to release the flavor of the spices.

7. Stir in the coconut, lemon zest and juice and coconut milk.

8. Correct the seasoning and serve the shrimp mixture in the crêpes.

Shrimp Newburg in Shells

4 SERVINGS

Ingredients

2 tbsp	oil	30 ml
2 tbsp	butter	30 ml
1 1/3 lb	peeled raw shrimp	600 g
4	mashed potatoes	4
1/2 cup	sherry **or** white wine	125 ml
1 1/2 cups	fish stock **or** shrimp (seafood) stock	375 ml
1 tbsp	butter	15 ml
1 tbsp	flour	15 ml
1/3 cup	35% cream	80 ml
1 tbsp	tomato paste	15 ml
	salt and freshly ground pepper to taste	

Method

1. In a skillet, heat the oil and melt the butter. Sauté the shrimp over high heat. Season to taste and set aside in shells or au gratin dishes. Garnish the edge of the shells or dishes with mashed potatoes.

2. Deglaze the skillet with the sherry and reduce by half.

3. Add the stock and bring to a boil.

4. In the meantime, combine the butter and flour to make a smooth paste. Whisk the paste into the hot liquid. Simmer until thickened.

5. Add the cream and tomato paste. Season to taste.

6. Spoon the sauce over the shrimp and place in the oven at 425°F (220°C) for 10 to 12 minutes.

Note:

The shrimp sauce may be served over pasta or rice or in *vol-au-vent* shells.

Scallop Brochettes with Honey

4 SERVINGS

I n g r e d i e n t s

24-30	scallops, cleaned	24-30
	vegetables of your choice, cut into pieces (peppers, onions, mushrooms, cherry tomatoes, zucchini, etc.)	
1/2 cup	oil	125 ml
1/4 cup	honey	60 ml
2	shallots, chopped	2
1 tbsp	mustard powder **or** Dijon mustard	15 ml
1 tbsp	your choice of chopped herbs (parsley, basil, thyme, oregano, etc.)	15 ml
	freshly ground pepper to taste	

Melon Salsa:

1/2 cup	diced honeydew melon	125 ml
1	shallot, chopped	1
3 tbsp	diced red pepper	45 ml
1/4 cup	oil	60 ml
1 tbsp	chopped fresh parsley	15 ml
1-2 tbsp	lime juice	15-30 ml
	salt and freshly ground pepper to taste	

M e t h o d

1. Make brochettes by alternately threading scallops and vegetable pieces onto the skewers.
2. Combine the oil, honey, shallots, mustard and herbs to make the marinade. Season with pepper to taste.
3. Marinate the brochettes for 1 to 2 hours in the refrigerator.
4. In the meantime, combine all the salsa ingredients and refrigerate.
5. Remove the brochettes from the marinade and set aside the marinade.
6. Cook on a preheated grill over medium-high heat for 3 to 4 minutes per side, basting with the marinade.
7. Serve the brochettes with the salsa.

Cocktail-Style Scallop en Papillote

Ingredients

Marinade:

1 tbsp	Dijon mustard	15 ml
1	clove garlic, chopped	1
1/2 tsp	chopped horseradish	2 ml
1	Italian tomato, diced	1
3 tbsp	white wine	45 ml
4	sprigs fresh thyme	4
4	lemon slices	4
	salt and freshly ground pepper to taste	
1 1/3 lb	cleaned scallops	600 g

Method

1. Combine all the marinade ingredients in a large bowl. Add the scallops and marinate for about 15 minutes.

2. Preheat the barbecue or oven to 400°F (200°C).

3. Cut four large pieces of aluminum foil and place a square of parchment paper in the center of each one to prevent the food from sticking.

4. Place one-quarter of the scallops on each square. Divide the marinade among the papillotes. Add as sprig of thyme and a lemon slice. Close the papillotes and seal tightly. Bake or barbecue for 10 to 12 minutes. Serve immediately.

Mushrooms Stuffed with Scallops

Ingredients

24	large white mushrooms	24
1/3 lb	softened cream cheese	150 g
2 tbsp	chopped chives	30 ml
2 tbsp	chopped parsley	30 ml
	salt and freshly ground pepper to taste	
24	scallops, cleaned	24

Method

1. Preheat the broiler.
2. Remove the stems from the mushrooms, scoop out a small cavity in each one and place cavity side up on a baking sheet.
3. In a food processor, combine the cheese, mushroom stems, chives and parsley and season to taste.
4. Stuff the mushrooms with the cheese and herb mixture.
5. Top with the scallops.
6. Bake in the broiler for 3 to 4 minutes, until the scallops are golden.
7. Serve hot or at room temperature.

Scallop Ceviche

Ingredients

1 lb	large, cleaned fresh scallops	450 g
3	lemons – juice	3
2	oranges – juice	2
1	shallot, chopped	1
2 tbsp	fresh herbs of your choice (parsley, basil, thyme, oregano, etc.)	30 ml
2 tbsp	minced red onion	30 ml
1 cup	julienned chayote	250 ml
1/2 cup	finely grated carrot	125 ml
1/4 cup	grated red cabbage	60 ml
1/4 cup	olive oil	60 ml
	salt and freshly ground pepper to taste	

Method

1. Slice the scallops into thirds horizontally.
2. In a bowl, combine the citrus juices, shallot and herbs. Add the sliced scallops. Cover and refrigerate 30 to 45 minutes, stirring three times.
3. Meanwhile, combine the vegetables in a bowl.
4. Drain the scallops, reserving the juice.
5. Stir in the oil and season to taste.
6. Pour half the juice over the vegetables and stir well. Divide into four servings.
7. Arrange the scallop slices on top of the vegetables and drizzle with the remaining juice. Garnish with orange slices and serve immediately.

Scallops
in Creamy Green Peppercorn-Papaya Sauce

4 SERVINGS

Ingredients

1 tbsp	butter	15 ml
1	shallot, chopped	1
1/2 cup	white wine	125 ml
1 1/3 cups	35% cream	330 ml
1	papaya, peeled, seeded and finely diced	1
1/2 tbsp	crushed green peppercorns	7 ml
	salt to taste	
2 tbsp	oil	30 ml
1 1/3 lb	large scallops, cleaned	600 g

Method

1. In a skillet, melt the butter and sauté the shallot.

2. Deglaze with the white wine and reduce by half.

3. Stir in the cream and simmer for 2 to 3 minutes.

4. Add the papaya, green peppercorns and salt to taste. Keep warm until the scallops are ready.

5. In a skillet, heat the oil over high heat and cook the scallops on one side only, without turning them. Continue cooking until the tops of the scallops start to turn opaque. Serve immediately, topped with the sauce accompanied with basmati rice and vegetables.

Index